MW00769443

T-REX
COLORING BOOK!

DISCOVER THIS UNIQUE COLLECTION OF COLORING PAGES

Bold Illustrations
COLORING BOOKS

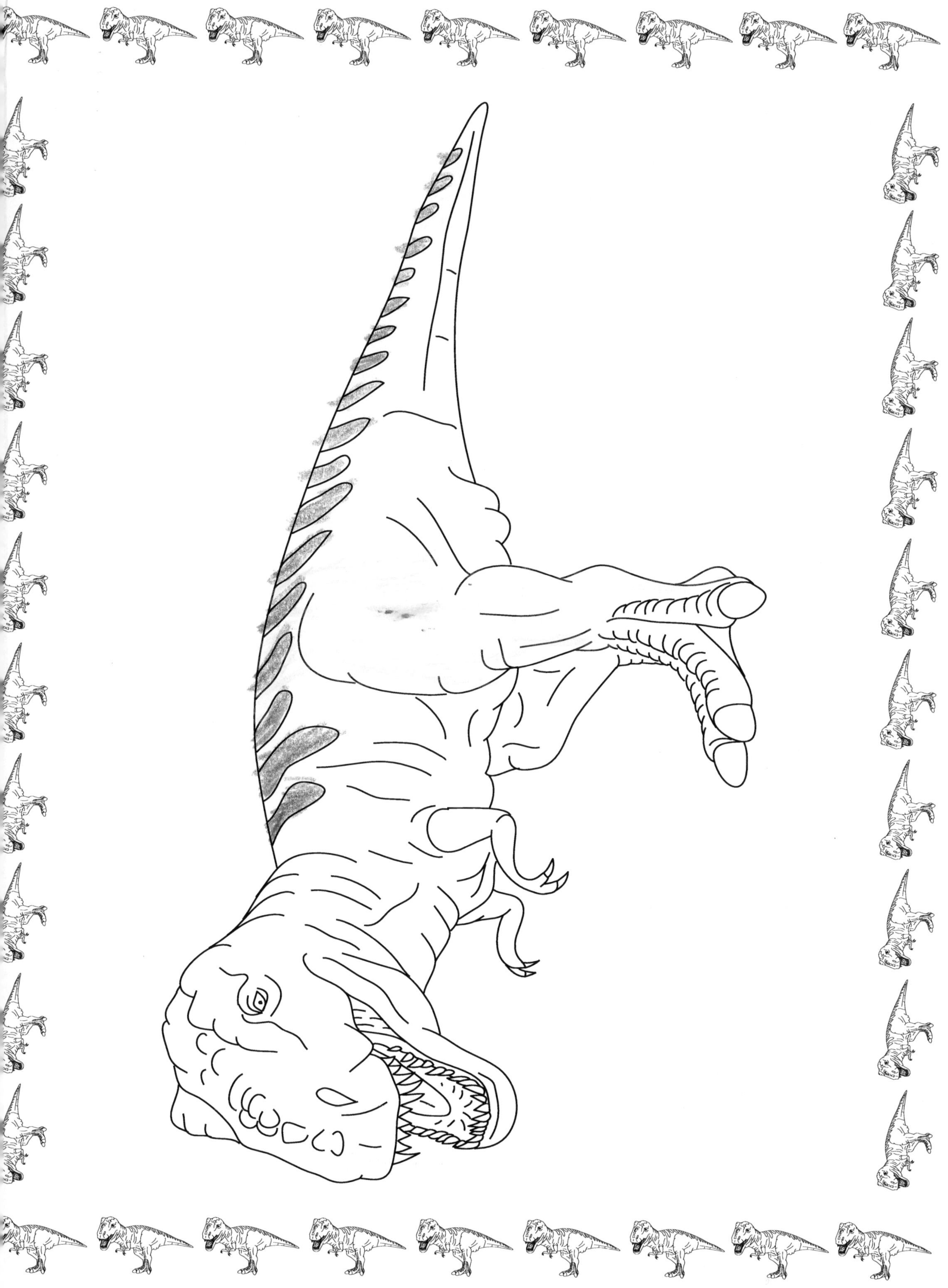

This is a Bleed Through Page If You Are Using a Colouring Marker or Pen!

Find Other Great Titles By searching for Bold Illustrations on Your Favorite Book Retailer

Amazon.Ca | Barnes & Noble (BN.Com) | Books A Million (BAM.Com)

Bold Illustrations

COLORING BOOKS

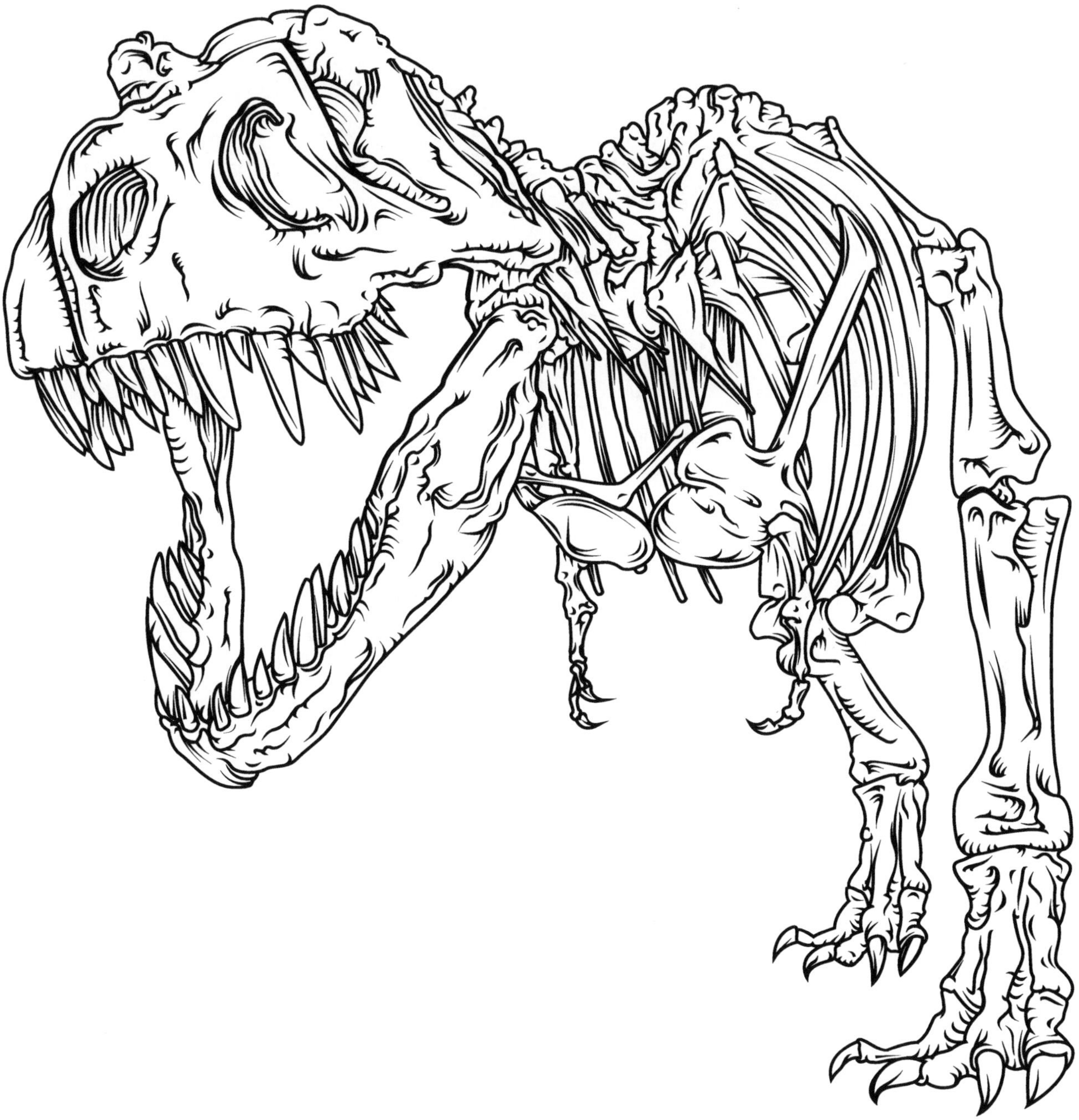

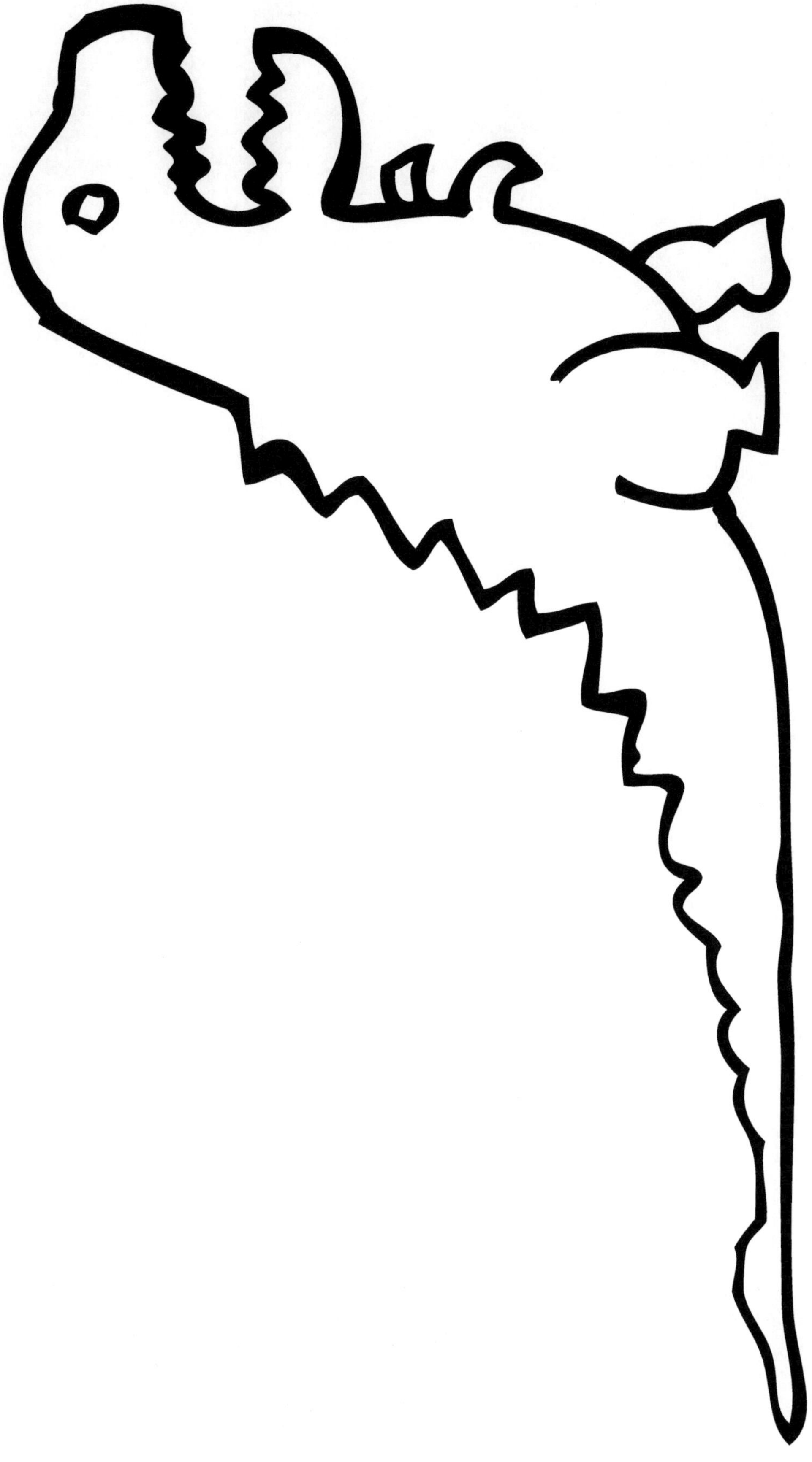

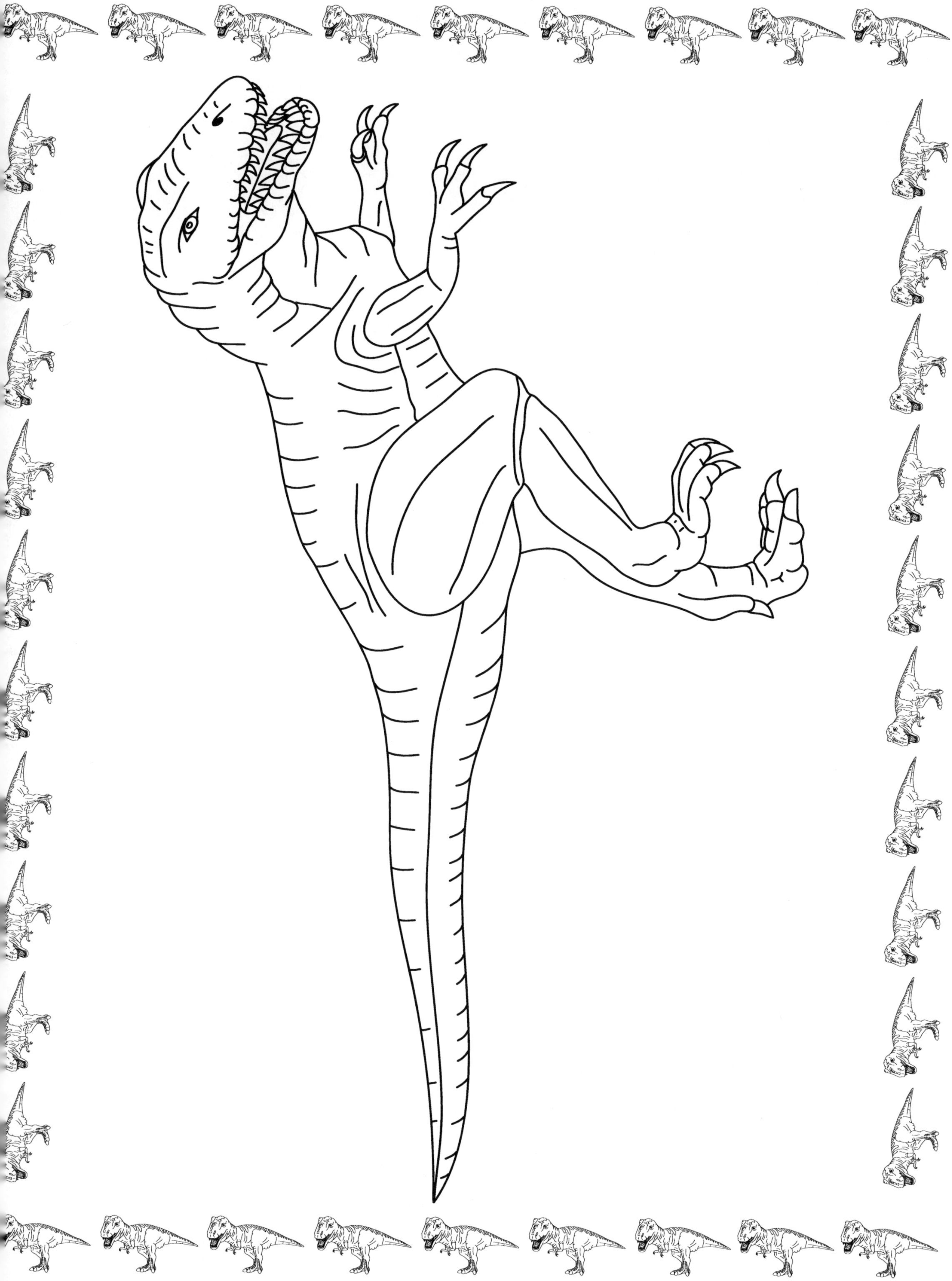

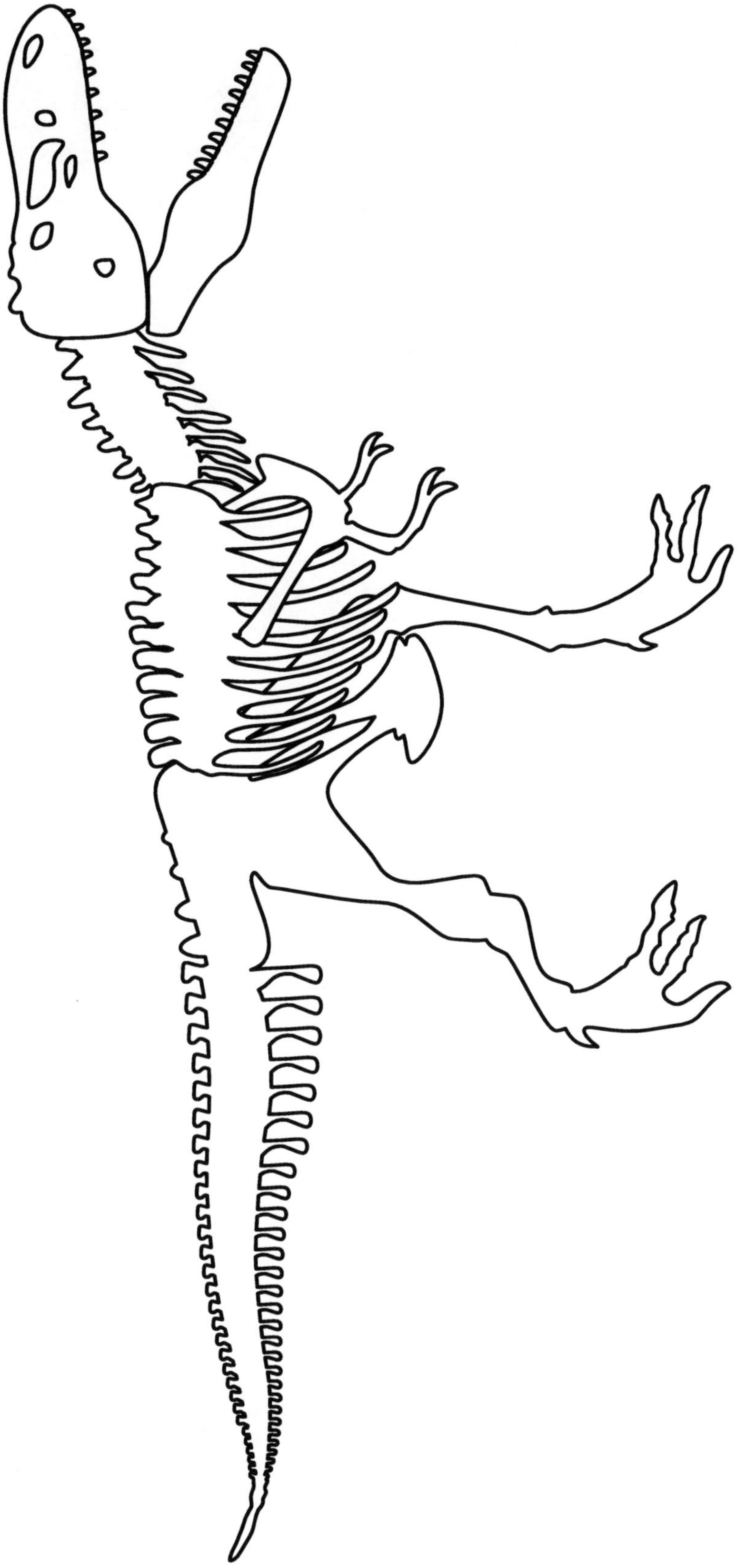

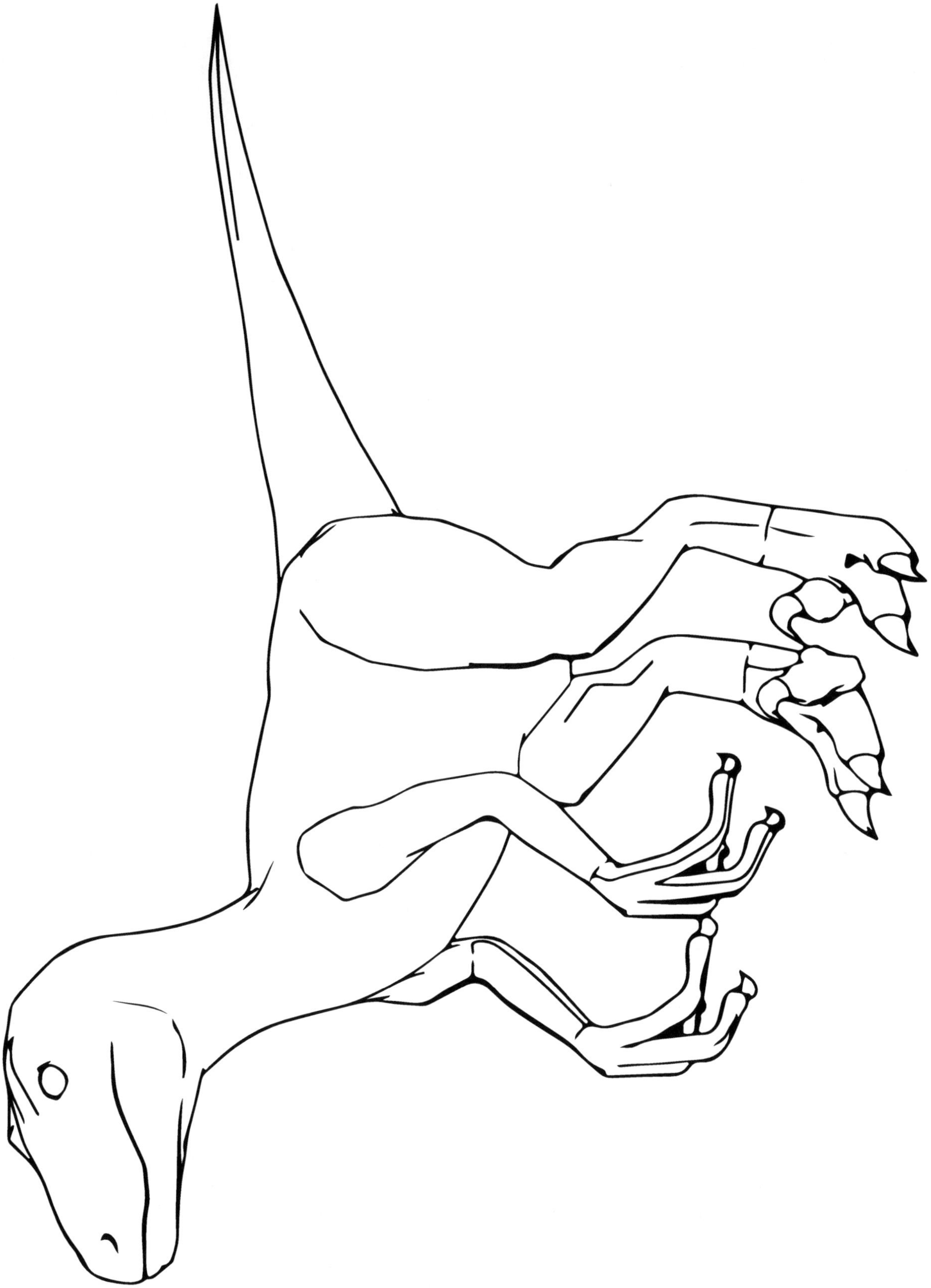

Made in the USA
Middletown, DE
06 February 2022

60611562R00033